never forget
facts & figures !

DOMINIC O'BRIEN

never forget facts & figures!

To all who wish to understand the
art and science of memory.

Never Forget!
Facts & Figures

Dominic O'Brien

First published in the United
Kingdom and Ireland in 2003 by
Duncan Baird Publishers Ltd
Sixth Floor
Castle House
75–76 Wells Street
London W1T 3QH

Conceived, created and designed
by Duncan Baird Publishers

British Library Cataloguing-in-
Publication Data:
A CIP record for this book is
available from the British Library.

ISBN: 1-904292-51-8

10 9 8 7 6 5 4 3 2

Typeset in Helvetica Condensed
Printed and bound in Thailand
by Imago

CONTENTS

USING MNEMONICS	14
THE ART OF ASSOCIATION	24
THE STORY METHOD	34
THE NUMBER–RHYME SYSTEM	44
THE NUMBER–SHAPE SYSTEM	56
THE MEMORY HOUSE	68
THE JOURNEY METHOD	80
THE DOMINIC SYSTEM	100
THE COMBINATION APPROACH	110

INTRODUCTION

Have you ever struggled to remember a fact or figure? Perhaps it was a famous date in history. Or maybe it was a song that hit number one, the name of a chemical compound or the capital of Sweden. Whatever it was, that particular fact or figure has buried itself deep within the vault of your memory and you just can't seem to retrieve it.

My advice is, don't put up with having an average memory. Improving your memory is a skill. If you master some basic techniques, remembering facts and figures can become a stimulating mental exercise – not to mention a chance to show off in conversation! Plus, a good memory for facts and figures can help you to sail through exams. ❯

People think that because I can remember so many facts and figures I must have a photographic memory. This isn't the case. There was a time when I struggled to remember 7 or 8 digits in a row, let alone 20 or 30 – and now I'm the 8-times winner of the World Memory Championships. I didn't just wake up one morning with the ability to remember. I simply studied the techniques for making my mind more supple and put them into practice. Here, I reveal these methods, sharing with you my specially-devised exercises that will help you never to forget facts and figures.

Dominic O'Brien

SYMBOLS USED IN THIS BOOK

 MEMORY TECHNIQUE

 MEMORY IN ACTION

 MEMORY WISDOM

WHY WE NEED TO REMEMBER FACTS AND FIGURES

Some people argue that there's no longer any need to commit facts and figures to memory. After all, if you've forgotten something, why not just look it up in a book or on the Internet? This is true – but I feel that there's still something invaluable about holding knowledge inside your >

head and about being able to refer to the specifics of a subject without the aid of a book or a computer. There are times when remembering facts and figures is critical – during exams, quizzes and presentations, for example.

The following techniques will help you to absorb facts and figures in an unhurried and interesting way – enabling you to retain them indefinitely.

USING MNEMONICS

One way to remember a fact or figure is to use a special device known as a mnemonic. Mnemonics convert boring, abstract or inaccessible information into something much more memory-friendly.

Some types of mnemonics involve rhyme. For example, everyone knows this mnemonic for remembering how many days

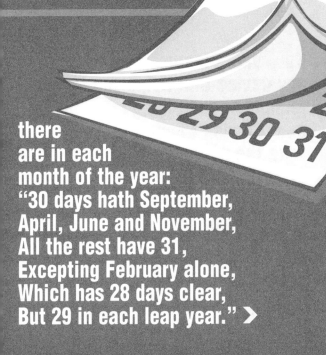

there
are in each
month of the year:
"30 days hath September,
April, June and November,
All the rest have 31,
Excepting February alone,
Which has 28 days clear,
But 29 in each leap year." ➤

However, a mnemonic can be any device that helps you to remember something more easily and it doesn't have to rhyme. Take the sentence: "Richard Of York Gave Battle In Vain", where the initial letters stand for Red, Orange, Yellow, Green, Blue, Indigo and Violet – the colours of the rainbow. If English history isn't

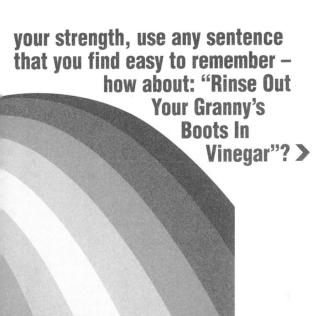

your strength, use any sentence that you find easy to remember – how about: "Rinse Out Your Granny's Boots In Vinegar"? ➤

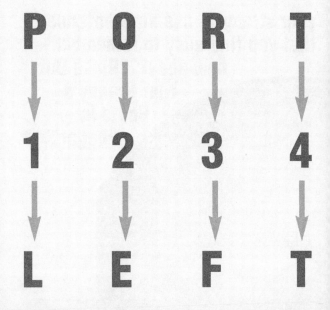

A mnemonic can also exploit the number of letters in a word – let's look at an example. Lots of people often forget that on a ship port is left and starboard is right. Conveniently, the word "port" contains four letters and so does the word "left". If we employ this mnemonic technique, suddenly the distinction is easy to remember!

HAVE A GO AT CREATING MNEMONICS FOR THE FOLLOWING
PIECES OF INFORMATION.

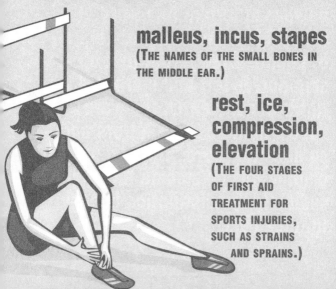

malleus, incus, stapes
(THE NAMES OF THE SMALL BONES IN
THE MIDDLE EAR.)

rest, ice, compression, elevation
(THE FOUR STAGES
OF FIRST AID
TREATMENT FOR
SPORTS INJURIES,
SUCH AS STRAINS
AND SPRAINS.)

Huron, Ontario, Michigan, Erie, Superior
(THE NAMES OF THE GREAT LAKES IN NORTH AMERICA.)

THE LATTER TWO EXAMPLES LEND THEMSELVES TO ACRONYM MNEMONICS — AN ACRONYM IS A WORD FORMED FROM THE INITIAL LETTERS OF OTHER WORDS. FOR THE FIRST AID TREATMENT YOU COULD IMAGINE TRIPPING OVER A HUGE BAG OF RICE AND SPRAINING YOUR ANKLE. FOR THE GREAT LAKES YOU COULD IMAGINE SUMMER HOMES ON THE BANKS OF THE LAKES. ALTERNATIVELY, YOU CAN DEVISE SENTENCE MNEMONICS. FOR EXAMPLE, MINUSCULE INNER SOUNDS (FOR MALLEUS, INCUS AND STAPES). A COMBINATION OF SENTENCE AND ACRONYM CAN WORK WELL FOR THE BONES OF THE INNER EAR. HOW ABOUT A GIRL SAYING "MR SPOCK, WHAT ARE THOSE ON THE SIDE OF YOUR HEAD?" HIS REPLY MIGHT BE "EARS, MIS".

A MENTAL WORK-OUT

Treat your brain like a muscle that needs a daily work-out to stay fit. Do crosswords, play chess, do arithmetic in your head and, at the end of each day, recall each event that happened to you in the correct sequence. These mental agility tasks will enhance the overall functioning of your memory.

THE ART OF ASSOCIATION

Our brains love things that are amusing, bizarre or visually exciting. If you can turn a boring fact or figure into an eccentric image in your head, you'll have no trouble remembering it. For this you will need to practise the art of association – the ability to look at a word or a number and turn it into a striking visual symbol.

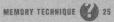

PRACTISE MAKING WORD ASSOCIATIONS AS OFTEN AS YOU CAN. ONE OF THE SIMPLEST WAYS OF DOING THIS IS THROUGH SOUND. WHEN ONE WORD SOUNDS LIKE ANOTHER YOU CAN OFTEN MAKE A MEMORABLE ASSOCIATION.

LOOK AT THE FOLLOWING LIST OF COUNTRIES AND WRITE DOWN ANY SOUND-ASSOCIATIONS THAT COME TO YOU.

Greece, Turkey, Jamaica, China, Cuba, Canada

THE ASSOCIATIONS THAT YOU MAKE FOR YOURSELF ARE THE BEST ONES BECAUSE THEY HAVE A UNIQUE AND PERSONAL QUALITY AND SO WILL BE THE MOST MEANINGFUL. BUT HERE ARE SOME OF MY ASSOCIATIONS TO HELP YOU GET STARTED.

For Greece I think of greasy oil; for Turkey I imagine the farmyard bird; for Jamaica, I think of someone making jam (the jam-maker); for China I see my favourite china ornament; for Cuba, I imagine a cube; and for Canada I picture a can.

If you struggle to come up with a meaningful association, use a technique called "part-wording" – taking the most striking syllable from a word and using it to form an association. Using "can" for "Canada" is an example of part-wording.

Tip: for some countries you may not need to use sound in your associations, a representative image may spring to mind instead – beer for Germany, perhaps, and a kangaroo for Australia. Always use the most natural and vivid association for you. ›

NOW THAT YOU'VE MADE VISUAL ASSOCIATIONS FOR THE
COUNTRIES IN THE LIST, YOU CAN MAKE
SIMILAR ASSOCIATIONS FOR THEIR CAPITAL CITIES.
SO IN ORDER:

> ATHENS – I THINK OF HENS
> ANKARA – I SEE AN ANCHOR
> KINGSTON – I IMAGINE THE KING OF A TOWN
> BEIJING – I THINK OF A PERSON BATHING
> HAVANA – GIVES ME THE GIRLS' NAME ANNA
> OTTAWA – PRESENTS AN OTTER

SOME OF THESE ASSOCIATIONS ARE "SOUND ALIKES".
FOR EXAMPLE, IT'S DIFFICULT TO PAIR A WORD SUCH AS
"BEIJING" WITH AN EVERYDAY OBJECT – AND ITS
COMPONENT SYLLABLES DON'T HELP US MUCH. SO A WORD,
SUCH AS "BATHING", THAT SOUNDS ROUGHLY SIMILAR TO
BEIJING, IS A GOOD COMPROMISE.

NOW CONNECT THE COUNTRIES TO THEIR CAPITALS BY FORMING LINKS BETWEEN THE ASSOCIATIONS. DON'T WORRY IF YOU COME UP WITH SOME SURREAL CONCOCTIONS. HERE ARE SOME EXAMPLES:

FOR GREECE AND ATHENS IMAGINE THROWING GREASE AT HENS; FOR TURKEY AND ANKARA IMAGINE A TURKEY WEIGHED DOWN BY AN ANCHOR; FOR JAMAICA AND KINGSTON IMAGINE THE KING OF A TOWN MAKING JAM; FOR CHINA AND BEIJING IMAGINE A CHINA FIGURE OF SOMEONE BATHING; FOR CUBA AND HAVANA IMAGINE A GIRL CALLED ANNA BALANCING ON A CUBE; FOR CANADA AND OTTAWA IMAGINE AN OTTER TRYING TO GET FOOD OUT OF A CAN.

HERE'S ANOTHER EXAMPLE OF HOW YOU CAN USE ASSOCIATIONS. LET'S SAY YOU ARE STUDYING CHEMISTRY AND YOU HAVE TROUBLE REMEMBERING THE SYMBOLS FOR CERTAIN ELEMENTS OF THE PERIODIC TABLE. SOME SYMBOLS, SUCH AS "H" FOR HYDROGEN, ARE STRAIGHTFORWARD, BUT THIS IS NOT SO FOR ALL OF THEM.

THE CHEMICAL SYMBOL FOR THE ELEMENT IRON IS "FE". WHAT ASSOCIATIONS CAN YOU MAKE FOR IRON? CAN THE LETTERS "FE" BE EXTENDED TO MAKE A MORE FAMILIAR WORD THAT CONJURES UP SOMETHING MEMORABLE — PERHAPS EVEN PLAYING ON OUR

EMOTIONS (WHICH HELP TO BRING THE CONNECTION ALIVE)?

WHEN I THINK OF IRON I THINK OF THE EXPRESSION "BEHIND IRON BARS", WHICH DESCRIBES BEING IN JAIL. AND I IMAGINE THAT IF I WERE IN JAIL I'D BE PRETTY FED UP.

WHAT ABOUT THE SYMBOL FOR SILVER, WHICH IS AG?

IN THIS CASE SILVER MAKES ME THINK OF A SILVER DENTAL FILLING I ONCE HAD. BEFORE I HAD THE FILLING I'D BEEN IN AGONY.

THINK LIKE A CHILD

When you make up associations you need to exploit your creativity to the full. This means undoing adult rules of rigid meanings and reverting to the fantasy thinking of childhood. Remember how a clothes horse made an excellent tent? Next time you look at an everyday object imagine all the possible functions it could have.

THE STORY METHOD

Think back to the fairy tales that you were told as a child. How easy is it to remember them now? I bet that, given a minute or so, you could accurately recall several. This is because stories excite our imagination, creating pictures in our minds and arousing us emotionally. As a result stories get hard-wired into our brains.

IF YOU CAN CREATE A STORY AROUND A SET OF FACTS YOU WILL BE ABLE TO EMBED FACTS DEEPLY IN YOUR MIND.

LET'S SAY THAT YOU WANT TO MEMORIZE THE PLANETS IN THEIR CORRECT ORDER FROM THE SUN:

Mercury, Venus, Earth, Mars, Jupiter, Saturn, Uranus, Neptune, Pluto

THE NAMES OF SOME PLANETS ARE EASY TO WEAVE INTO A STORY BECAUSE THEY'RE READILY ASSOCIATED WITH OBJECTS

(FOR EXAMPLE, MERCURY AND A THERMOMETER), OR EVEN A PART OF THE BODY (URANUS, FOR EXAMPLE — IT MIGHT BE RUDE BUT YOU'LL REMEMBER IT!). OTHER PLANETS ARE LESS EASY, BUT YOU CAN USE RHYME AS A CUE (FOR EXAMPLE, MARS AND STARS) OR BREAK UP THE SYLLABLES TO MAKE THEM

MEANINGFUL (SATURN CAN BECOME SAT ON AN URN). IN SOME CASES, SUCH AS JUPITER, YOU'RE FORCED TO BE REALLY CREATIVE. I MIGHT USE A SKIRT TO REPRESENT JUPITER BECAUSE "JUPE" IN FRENCH MEANS SKIRT, BUT YOU CAN COME UP WITH YOUR OWN IDEAS.›

HERE'S A POSSIBLE OPENING TO YOUR PLANET STORY:

Mercury was having his temperature taken by a beautiful woman called Venus.
"You're too ill to stay on Earth," she said. **"You must travel all the way through the stars to Mars."**

— NOW YOU FINISH THE STORY.

You can use the Story Method for any lists that are too dry or abstract to recall without effort. For example, you might need to remember a list of muscles for an anatomy exam. It's worth spending time creating strong associations that you weave into a story because once you've rehearsed them a few times they will be securely lodged in your mind. ❯

EVEN THE BAFFLING NAMES OF CHEMICALS CAN BE MADE ACCESSIBLE IF YOU TAKE THE TIME TO BREAK THEM DOWN AND TURN THE COMPONENTS INTO A STORY.

TAKE THE EXAMPLE OF

adenosine triphosphate –

THE CHEMICAL FORM IN WHICH ENERGY IS STORED INSIDE OUR BODY.

YOUR FRIEND **ADE** HAS SHOWN A GREAT DEAL OF **NOSINE**SS ABOUT YOUR **TRIP** TO **HOSP**ITAL — WHICH YOU **HATE**.

AND AS AN ADDITIONAL MEMORY CUE YOU CAN MAKE THE REASON FOR YOUR HOSPITAL VISIT A CHRONIC LACK OF **ENERGY**.

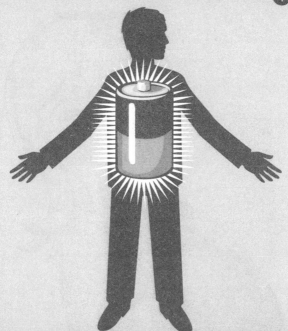

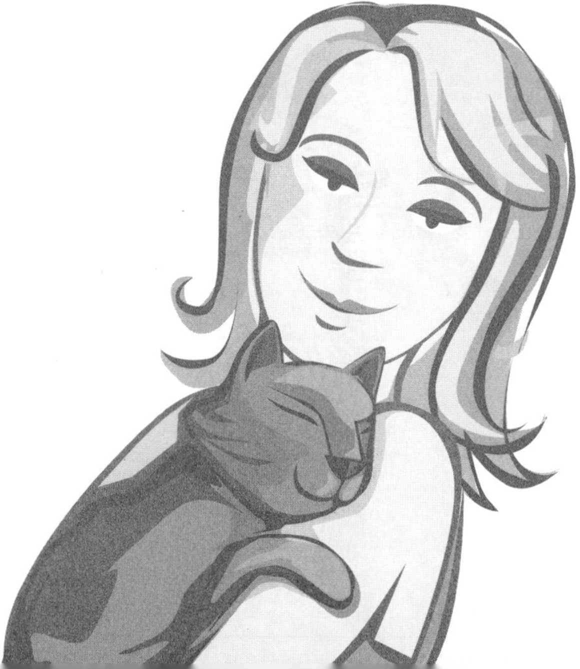

PERSONALIZE YOUR AIDS

When you make up mnemonics, tailor them to your tastes or to your sense of humour. If you're an animal lover, populate your memory aids with cats and dogs. If rude mnemonics appeal to you, be as risqué as you like – after all you don't have have to share them with anyone.

THE NUMBER–RHYME SYSTEM

Numbers are naturally difficult to remember. They're abstract things, devoid of mood, colour and emotion. We already know that words are much more interesting. Through them we can create strings of memorable associations. So, the best way to make numbers easy to remember is to turn them into words.

START BY THINKING OF A WORD THAT RHYMES WITH EACH NUMBER FROM 0 TO 9. HERE ARE SOME SUGGESTIONS:

0 – a hero

1 – a bun, a nun or the sun

2 – a shoe or some glue

3 – a tree, a bee or a knee

4 – a door, a saw or a paw

5 – a hive or a dive

6 – some sticks or bricks

7 – heaven

8 – a gate, a date or a weight

9 – some wine, a line or
     a sign

TIP: WHEN YOU THINK OF WORDS TO RHYME WITH
NUMBERS, CHOOSE NOUNS (WORDS DESCRIBING THINGS
OR PLACES) RATHER THAN VERBS (WORDS THAT DESCRIBE
ACTIONS) OR ADJECTIVES (WORDS THAT DESCRIBE NOUNS).
NOUNS ARE EASIER TO VISUALIZE THAN ANY OTHER TYPE
OF WORD AND YOU CAN INCORPORATE THEM MORE EASILY
INTO ASSOCIATIONS AND STORIES. >

GET INTO THE HABIT OF PAIRING NUMBERS WITH THEIR RHYMING WORDS IN YOUR DAY-TO-DAY LIFE, EVEN WHEN YOU'RE NOT TRYING TO MEMORIZE THINGS. LET'S SAY YOU VISIT NUMBER 59 IN A ROW OF HOUSES. INVENT A LITTLE SCENE FOR YOURSELF AS YOU MAKE YOUR WAY THERE. FOR EXAMPLE, YOU COULD IMAGINE A DOOR OPENING TO REVEAL A COMPLETE DIVE (FIVE) WITH PEOPLE LYING AROUND DRINKING WINE (NINE) OUT OF BOTTLES.

NOW TRY TO APPLY NUMBER–RHYMES
TO A FACT THAT YOU WANT TO LEARN.

SUPPOSING THAT
YOU'VE GOT A HUMAN
BIOLOGY TEST COMING
UP AND YOU NEED TO
REMEMBER THAT THE
RESTING HUMAN HEART
BEATS AN AVERAGE OF 70
TIMES A MINUTE.

YOU COULD IMAGINE THAT WHEN YOU
DIE AND YOUR HEART STOPS BEATING
YOU GO TO HEAVEN (SEVEN) WHERE
YOU FINALLY GET TO MEET ALL YOUR
HEROES (ZERO). >

PERHAPS YOU'RE GOING TO A POP QUIZ. HOW WOULD YOU MEMORIZE THE FACT THAT THE BEATLES' DEBUT SONG ("LOVE ME DO") WAS RECORDED IN 1962?

YOU DON'T NEED TO MEMORIZE THE "19" BECAUSE YOU KNOW THAT THE BEATLES FORMED IN THE 20TH CENTURY. SO, YOU COULD IMAGINE THAT THE BEATLES ARE BEATING TIME TO "LOVE ME DO" BY BANGING STICKS (SIX) ON A SHOE (TWO). ›

MAYBE YOU JUST WANT TO MEMORIZE SOME
UNUSUAL FACTS TO DROP INTO CONVERSATION.
FOR EXAMPLE, THE MAXIMUM LIFESPAN OF A
HEDGEHOG IS 14 YEARS (IMAGINE A HEDGEHOG
EATING A BUN [ONE] WITH ITS PAW [FOUR]),
WHEREAS THE MAXIMUM LIFESPAN OF A
GIRAFFE IS 36 (IMAGINE A GIRAFFE GOING UP
TO A TREE [THREE] AND CHEWING ON SOME
STICKS [SIX]).

IF YOU WERE GIVING A TALK ON THE DANGERS OF SMOKING, HOW WOULD YOU REMEMBER THE FACT THAT 62 MILLION PEOPLE SMOKE IN THE US? ONE WAY WOULD BE TO IMAGINE STICKS (SIX), INSTEAD OF CIGARETTES, BEING STUBBED OUT UNDER A SHOE (TWO) — A MILLION TIMES.

TRY APPLYING NUMBER—RHYMES TO SOME FIGURES THAT YOU WANT TO REMEMBER.

BREATHE ... RELAX ... REMEMBER

The enemy of memory is stress. If you're trying to recall a fact or figure while you're fretting about something else, your memory will fail you. Take a minute to breathe in and breathe out slowly and deliberately. Silently repeat the word "calm" as you breathe. Once your mind is settled, your memory will not falter.

THE NUMBER–SHAPE SYSTEM

As I've said, there's something intrinsically uninspiring about numbers. We need to make them more exciting. A good way to do this is to take the shape of a number and imagine all the things that it reminds us of. If you are one of those people who think in a highly visual way, you'll find this technique especially useful.

THE FIRST STEP IN THE NUMBER–SHAPE SYSTEM IS TO PAIR EACH NUMBER FROM ZERO TO NINE WITH AN ITEM THAT RESEMBLES THE SHAPE OF THE DIGIT. HERE ARE SOME SUGGESTIONS:

0 – ANYTHING ROUND, SUCH AS A TENNIS BALL OR A SNOWBALL.

1 – ANYTHING STRAIGHT AND VERTICAL, SUCH AS A CANDLE, A PENCIL OR A ROCKET.

2 – A SWAN, OR A SNAKE ABOUT TO STRIKE.

3 – A PAIR OF PUCKERED LIPS.

4 – A FLAG ON A FLAG POLE OR AN UNFURLED SAIL ON A BOAT.

5 – A GRACEFUL SEAHORSE OR AN
S-SHAPED HOOK.

6 – AN ELEPHANT'S TRUNK OR A
GOLF CLUB.

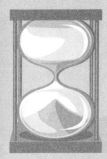

7 – A BOOMERANG OR THE
EDGE OF A CLIFF.

8 – A SNOWMAN OR AN
HOURGLASS.

9 – A BALLOON ON A
RIBBON.

ONCE YOU'VE MADE NUMBER–SHAPE PAIRS THAT YOU'RE
HAPPY WITH (YOU DON'T HAVE TO USE MY SUGGESTIONS),
YOU'RE READY TO APPLY THE TECHNIQUE. ›

HERE ARE SOME FACTS AND FIGURES THAT I'D LIKE YOU TO
MEMORIZE USING NUMBER-SHAPES. YOU NEED TO THINK OF
AN IMAGE THAT GIVES YOU A CLUE TO THE SUBJECT AND
THEN COMBINE IT WITH THE RELEVANT NUMBER-SHAPE.

THE HUMAN HEART
HAS 4 CHAMBERS.

ON THE BEAUFORT
WIND SCALE, 9 IS A
STRONG GALE.

A DODECAHEDRON HAS 12 PLANE FACES.

AN AVERAGE GLASS OF WHITE WINE CONTAINS 80 CALORIES.

THE ATOMIC NUMBER OF CARBON IS 6.

THE FIRST WOMAN TO CLIMB MOUNT EVEREST DID SO IN 1975. >

How did you get on? Here are some ways in which you could have visualized these facts and figures.

A flag (the number–shape for 4) bearing a big red heart is being raised up a flag pole.

A balloon tied by a piece of string (the number–shape for 9) to a fence is being blown around in a strong gale.

You can dimly see a large object in front of you so you light a candle (the number–shape for 1) to see better. There before you is an enormous dodecahedron with a single black snake (the number–shape for 2) slithering across it. >

A SNOWMAN (THE NUMBER–SHAPE FOR 8) IS ABOUT TO TAKE A SIP FROM A GLASS OF WINE WHEN SOMEONE THROWS A SNOWBALL (THE NUMBER–SHAPE FOR 0) AT HIM.

SOMEONE HAS SET FIRE TO YOUR GOLF CLUBS (THE NUMBER—SHAPE FOR 6)! YOU GO TO INSPECT THE DAMAGE BUT ONLY CARBON REMAINS.

A WOMAN STOPS ON A CLIFF EDGE (THE NUMBER—SHAPE FOR 7) HALF WAY UP MOUNT EVEREST. SHE IS WEARING A SPECIAL SEAHORSE CHARM (THE NUMBER—SHAPE FOR 5), FOR GOOD LUCK.

GO RUNNING

When I'm in training for a competition I always make time to go for a morning run. Any aerobic exercise such as running, swimming, cycling or fast walking gets blood pumping round the body and gives the brain a big oxygen boost. There's no better way to wake you up and improve mental clarity and your memory.

THE MEMORY HOUSE

Memories, like household objects, need to be stored in a safe place. If you know where to find them, they are effortless to retrieve. Many memory techniques, such as the story method, involve imagination and association, but if you use location as well, you create very strong memories that can't easily be dislodged from your mind.

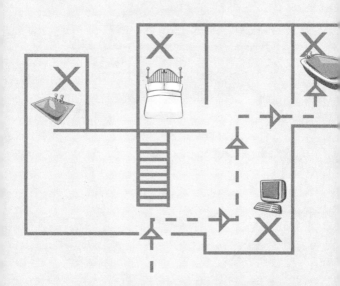

WHAT IS THE PLACE THAT YOU KNOW BEST? FOR MOST OF US IT'S OUR HOME. WE KNOW THE LAYOUT OF THE ROOMS INTIMATELY AND THIS MAKES THE HOME AN IDEAL PLACE IN WHICH TO "STORE" ITEMS THAT WE WANT TO REMEMBER.

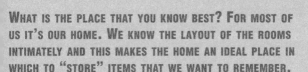

LET'S START SIMPLY. TAKE A MENTAL TOUR OF YOUR HOUSE. IMAGINE WALKING THOUGH THE FRONT DOOR. WHICH ROOM DO YOU COME TO FIRST? WALK THROUGH EACH ROOM IN SEQUENCE UNTIL YOU HAVE MENTALLY VISITED THEM ALL. FOR EACH ROOM TRY TO IDENTIFY THREE KEY PLACES WHERE YOU COULD STORE ITEMS THAT YOU WANT TO REMEMBER — PLACES SUCH AS THE KITCHEN SINK, THE BOOKSHELVES IN YOUR STUDY, AND SO ON. >

LET'S SAY THAT YOU HAVE A NUTRITION TEST COMING UP AND YOU NEED TO REMEMBER THREE FOODS THAT ARE RICH SOURCES OF THE MINERALS IRON, ZINC, CALCIUM AND POTASSIUM.

Iron: liver, dried beans, apricots

Zinc: oysters, beef, peanuts

Calcium: milk, cheese, canned sardines

Potassium: salmon, spinach, bananas

IN THIS CASE, YOU HAVE TWO SETS OF FACTS TO REMEMBER — THE FOUR DIFFERENT MINERALS AND THE THREE FOODS THAT ARE RICH IN EACH MINERAL. IT'S A GOOD IDEA TO GROUP YOUR LOCATIONS. START BY SELECTING FOUR SPECIFIC ROOMS AND ALLOCATE EACH OF THE FOUR MINERALS TO A ROOM. FOR EXAMPLE, YOU COULD PUT IRON IN THE BEDROOM, ZINC IN THE BATHROOM, POTASSIUM IN THE KITCHEN AND CALCIUM IN THE STUDY. THESE ARE MY SUGGESTIONS — YOU CAN MAKE UP YOUR OWN. >

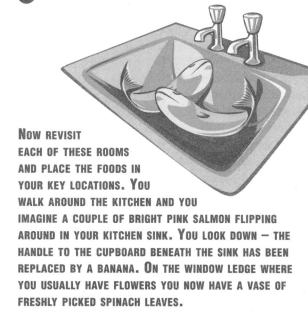

NOW REVISIT
EACH OF THESE ROOMS
AND PLACE THE FOODS IN
YOUR KEY LOCATIONS. YOU
WALK AROUND THE KITCHEN AND YOU
IMAGINE A COUPLE OF BRIGHT PINK SALMON FLIPPING
AROUND IN YOUR KITCHEN SINK. YOU LOOK DOWN – THE
HANDLE TO THE CUPBOARD BENEATH THE SINK HAS BEEN
REPLACED BY A BANANA. ON THE WINDOW LEDGE WHERE
YOU USUALLY HAVE FLOWERS YOU NOW HAVE A VASE OF
FRESHLY PICKED SPINACH LEAVES.

IN THE STUDY, YOUR COMPUTER SCREENSAVER SHOWS MULTIPLE CANS OF SARDINES GLIDING ACROSS THE SCREEN, YOUR MOUSE IS MADE FROM A ROUND PIECE OF CHEESE AND YOUR BOOKSHELVES ARE FILLED WITH ROWS AND ROWS OF NEATLY STACKED MILK CARTONS INSTEAD OF BOOKS. ❯

ON ENTERING THE BATHROOM, YOU NOTICE THAT THE BATH TUB FEATURES AN EXTRAVAGANT DISPLAY OF SHELLFISH, WITH A CENTREPIECE OF BEAUTIFULLY ARRANGED OYSTERS. A TORRENT OF PEANUTS FALL ON YOUR HEAD AS YOU OPEN THE MEDICINE CABINET AND A BIG, JUICY STEAK IS DRAPED OVER THE RAIL WHERE THE TOWEL USUALLY HANGS.

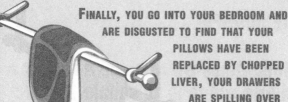

FINALLY, YOU GO INTO YOUR BEDROOM AND ARE DISGUSTED TO FIND THAT YOUR PILLOWS HAVE BEEN REPLACED BY CHOPPED LIVER, YOUR DRAWERS ARE SPILLING OVER WITH DRIED KIDNEY, LIMA AND BUTTER BEANS AND YOUR CARPET IS STREWN WITH FRESH APRICOTS THAT YOU CAN'T AVOID TREADING ON.

ONCE YOU HAVE FILED EACH ITEM IN YOUR HOUSE, WAIT AN HOUR BEFORE RETRACING YOUR STEPS AND TRYING TO RECALL THEM. REHEARSE A COUPLE OF TIMES MORE IF YOU NEED TO. APPLY THE SAME TECHNIQUE TO OTHER FACTS THAT YOU WOULD LIKE TO REMEMBER.

BE MINDFUL

Sometimes we're given a fact or a figure which is so simple that we don't focus upon it fully in order to retain it. Then, hey presto, later in the day that "simple" fact or figure has vanished. Why? We didn't give it our full attention. Even when you think something will be easy to recall, make a conscious effort to store it.

THE JOURNEY METHOD

The Journey Method is my very own adaptation of the Memory House Method. The beauty of it is that, whereas I'm 100 per cent familiar with only one house, I can confidently recall several journeys. This gives me plenty of scope for memorization. Also, because the Journey Method uses a specific "route", it is ideal for memorizing items in a set order.

START BY CHOOSING ONE JOURNEY THAT YOU KNOW WELL,
PERHAPS FROM HOME TO WORK OR WORK TO THE GYM.
IDENTIFY 15 SIGNIFICANT LANDMARKS THAT YOU COME TO
ALONG THE WAY. YOU CAN EXPAND THIS NUMBER LATER IF
YOU NEED TO.

NOW THAT YOU HAVE 15 LANDMARKS,
YOU CAN MEMORIZE 15 FACTS.

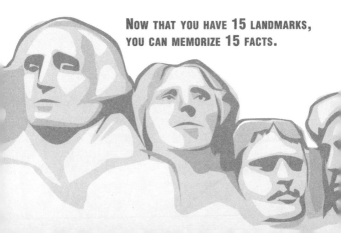

LET'S SAY THAT YOU WANT TO LEARN THE NAMES OF THE LAST 15 US PRESIDENTS, STARTING WITH THE MOST RECENT. IMAGINE THAT YOU ARE WALKING ALONG YOUR ROUTE. AS YOU COME TO YOUR FIRST LANDMARK, MAKE UP A SCENE OR A STORY TO ASSOCIATE IT WITH THE FIRST PRESIDENT ON YOUR LIST. AS YOU GET TO THE SECOND LANDMARK DO THE SAME WITH THE SECOND PRESIDENT ... AND SO ON. HERE ARE THE 15 PRESIDENTS:

GEORGE W. BUSH
BILL CLINTON
GEORGE BUSH
RONALD REAGAN
JIMMY CARTER
GERALD FORD
RICHARD NIXON
LYNDON B. JOHNSON

JOHN F. KENNEDY
DWIGHT D. EISENHOWER
HARRY S. TRUMAN
FRANKLIN D. ROOSEVELT
HERBERT HOOVER
CALVIN COOLIDGE
WARREN HARDING >

I'M GOING TO GIVE YOU SOME EXAMPLES OF POSSIBLE
SCENARIOS FOR THE FIRST FIVE PRESIDENTS — THEN YOU
CAN TRY THE REST YOURSELF. THE FIRST FIVE LOCATIONS
ON MY JOURNEY ARE THE FRONT LAWN, THE BANK, A CAKE
STORE, A LAUNDROMAT AND A FRUIT STAND.

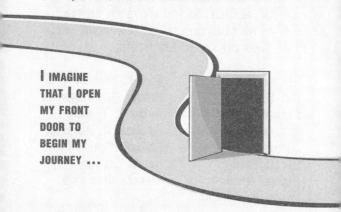

I IMAGINE
THAT I OPEN
MY FRONT
DOOR TO
BEGIN MY
JOURNEY ...

STRAIGHT AWAY I SEE GEORGE W. BUSH ON MY FRONT LAWN. TO MAKE THE ASSOCIATION, I IMAGINE THAT HE IS CLIPPING THE HEDGE (A BUSH!) INTO THE SHAPE OF THE LETTERS G AND W.

I WALK ON AND COME TO THE BANK. HERE BILL CLINTON IS COUNTING OUT DOLLAR BILLS ON THE FRONT STEPS. ❯

NEXT I COME TO A CAKE STORE WHERE GEORGE BUSH IS
GORGING ON ENORMOUS CREAM CAKES.

I WALK A LITTLE FURTHER UNTIL
I REACH RONALD REAGAN IN THE
LAUNDROMAT. I IMAGINE
HIM POINTING A **RAY
GUN** AT A
FAULTY MACHINE.

THEN I PASS A FRUIT STAND WHERE JIMMY CARTER IS SELLING APPLES FROM A **CART** WITH THE WORD **"JIMMY'S"** PAINTED ON IT IN LARGE BRIGHT LETTERS.

... AND SO ON. NOW YOU TRY — USE YOUR OWN **15**-STAGE JOURNEY FOR MEMORIZING THE PRESIDENTS.

REMEMBER TO ADD AN IMAGINATIVE ASSOCIATION THAT LINKS THE PRESIDENT WITH THE PLACE.

YOU CAN ALSO USE THE JOURNEY METHOD FOR
MEMORIZING NUMBERS. TRY THIS EXERCISE TO SEE HOW.
TRY MEMORIZING THE POPULATIONS OF THE FOLLOWING
FIVE COUNTRIES:

USA – 266 MILLION PEOPLE
GERMANY – 76 MILLION PEOPLE
UK – 58 MILLION PEOPLE
AUSTRALIA – 19 MILLION PEOPLE
NORWAY – 4 MILLION PEOPLE

19

START BY THINKING OF OBJECTS THAT REMIND YOU OF THE COUNTRIES – JUST AS YOU DID ON PAGE 27. THEN, SIMPLIFY THE FIGURES. YOU KNOW THAT THE POPULATIONS ARE ALL IN THE MILLIONS SO YOU DON'T NEED TO BOTHER MEMORIZING THE ZEROS. NEXT, CHOOSE WHETHER YOU'RE GOING TO USE THE NUMBER-SHAPE SYSTEM OR THE NUMBER-RHYME SYSTEM TO MEMORIZE THE NUMBERS. NOW CHOOSE A JOURNEY, IDENTIFY FIVE LANDMARKS AND CREATE SCENES TO LINK TOGETHER THE COUNTRIES, THE NUMBERS AND THE LANDMARKS. >

How did you do? If you found this exercise difficult, take a look at the way I'd do it.

I've chosen to use the Number–Shape system. The landmarks on my journey are going to be a large detached house, a liquor store, a women's clothes store, a park and a travel agent.

I start my journey and quickly come to my first landmark – the large detached house. For the US I think of "us" – my family. I imagine us all hanging out of the windows of the house screaming. Why? Because a snake (the number–shape for 2) is slithering up the front lawn followed by two enormous elephants swinging their trunks (the number–shapes for 6). >

Now I arrive at the liquor store. As I associate Germany with beer, I picture the liquor store hosting a beer tasting. Amid all the activity a boomerang (the number-shape for 7) is thrown to an elephant who is guzzling beer through his trunk (the number-shape for 6).

I WALK ON UNTIL I REACH THE WOMEN'S CLOTHES STORE. IN THE WINDOW DISPLAY THE FIRST OF THREE MANNEQUINS IS WEARING A UNION JACK (MY SYMBOL FOR THE UK) T-SHIRT. THE SECOND IS WEARING A DRESS WITH A SEAHORSE (THE NUMBER–SHAPE FOR 5) MOTIF AND THE THIRD IS UNDRESSED TO REVEAL A PERFECT HOUR-GLASS (THE NUMBER–SHAPE FOR 8) FIGURE. >

NEXT I GET TO THE PARK. MY SYMBOL FOR AUSRALIA IS A KANGAROO. I SEE A KANGAROO THAT HAS LOST ITS HOP! IT'S TRYING TO LAUNCH ITSELF INTO THE AIR USING A ROCKET (THE NUMBER-SHAPE FOR 1) BUT KEEPS FAILING. IT GIVES UP AND ATTACHES ITSELF TO A GIGANTIC BALLOON ON A PIECE OF STRING (THE NUMBER-SHAPE FOR 9) AND FLOATS THROUGH THE AIR.

MY FINAL LANDMARK IS THE TRAVEL AGENT. MY SYMBOL FOR NORWAY IS MY BANK MANAGER, NORMAN. I IMAGINE HIM BOOKING A YACHTING HOLIDAY (THE SAIL IS THE NUMBER-SHAPE FOR 4), PAID FOR WITH THE INTEREST EARNED ON MY ACCOUNT!

A PORTFOLIO OF JOURNEYS

Once you've got the hang of the Journey Method, try to create a portfolio of journeys in which you can store information. It's a good idea to keep several "empty" journeys in mind – ones in which you've identified key landmarks. In this way, if you're presented with some new information you instantly have a place to store it.

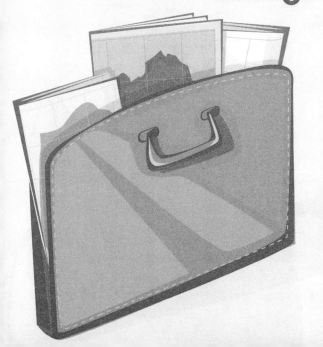

BRAIN FOOD

Nicknamed "brain food", oily fish is rich in folic acid and contains several essential fatty acids – all of which are crucial for maintaining a healthy brain and nervous system. Eat plenty of oily fish to ensure optimum memory performance. Bananas, red peppers and spinach are also good memory-boosting foods.

THE DOMINIC SYSTEM

The final memory technique that I'd like to explain is the DOMINIC system. DOMINIC stands for Decipherment Of Mnemonically Interpreted Numbers Into Characters and it's a world-class technique that I have personally devised for use in competitions. It has enabled me to remember hundreds of facts and figures.

THE FIRST STEP OF THE **DOMINIC** SYSTEM IS TO PAIR
EACH NUMBER FROM 0 TO 9 WITH A LETTER AS FOLLOWS:

0 – O
1 – A
2 – B
3 – C
4 – D

5 – E
6 – S
7 – G
8 – H
9 – N

IF YOU'RE WONDERING ABOUT THE RATIONALE BEHIND MY CHOICE OF NUMBER–LETTER PAIRS, IT'S SIMPLE. A IS THE FIRST LETTER OF THE ALPHABET SO I'VE PAIRED 1 WITH A. NUMBERS 2 TO 5 AND 7 AND 8 ARE ALSO PAIRED WITH THE LETTER THAT MATCHES THEIR POSITION IN THE ALPHABET. I CHOSE THE LETTER O TO REPRESENT ZERO BECAUSE THEY BOTH LOOK THE SAME. I CHOSE THE LETTER S TO REPRESENT 6 BECAUSE SIX HAS A STRONG "S" SOUND. AND I CHOSE N AND 9 BECAUSE THE WORD NINE CONTAINS TWO "N"S. >

THE NEXT THING I DO IN THE **DOMINIC** SYSTEM IS TO TRANSLATE ALL THE NUMBERS FROM 0 TO 99 INTO PAIRS OF LETTERS.

INCIDENTALLY, TO MAKE ALL THE NUMBERS TRANSLATE INTO NEAT PAIRS, I PUT A 0 IN FRONT OF SINGLE NUMBERS. FOR EXAMPLE, 00, 01, 02 AND SO ON. THIS MEANS THAT I END UP WITH A HUNDRED LETTER PAIRS.

HERE'S A SELECTION TO GIVE YOU THE IDEA:

00 is OO
07 is OG
14 is AD

21 is BA
28 is BH ›

NEXT I CONVERT THESE LETTER PAIRS INTO ACTUAL PEOPLE'S INITIALS (EITHER PEOPLE I KNOW IN MY PERSONAL LIFE OR FAMOUS PEOPLE). THIS IS THE STRENGTH OF THE **DOMINIC** SYSTEM: INSTEAD OF BEING DRY AND ABSRACT, EVERY NUMBER FROM 0 TO 99 SUDDENLY

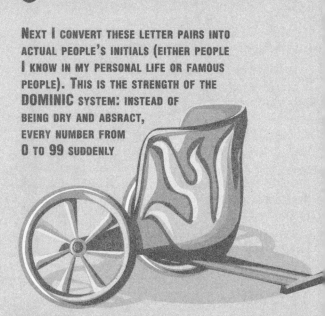

HAS A FACE, A PERSONALITY, AN OCCUPATION
AND A SET OF UNIQUE ASSOCIATIONS IN
MY MIND.

NUMBERS COME ALIVE, AND
ARE INTERESTING AND EASY
TO REMEMBER. HERE ARE
SOME EXAMPLES:

Clint Eastwood – 35
Charlton Heston – 38
Donald Duck – 44
Steven Spielberg – 66
George Orwell – 70 ›

NOW IT'S TIME TO APPLY THE **DOMINIC** SYSTEM TO SOME FIGURES THAT YOU WANT TO REMEMBER. IMAGINE THAT YOU WOULD LIKE TO MEMORIZE THE NUMBER OF UMBRELLAS HANDED IN LAST YEAR TO THE NEW YORK SUBWAY LOST PROPERTY OFFICE — LET'S SAY THE FIGURE IS 8,348. FIRST, SPLIT THE NUMBER UP INTO PAIRS OF DIGITS: 83 AND 48. THEN CONVERT THEM TO INITIALS: HC AND DH. NOW IMAGINE THAT HILARY CLINTON AND DARYL HANNAH ARE GETTING OFF A SUBWAY

TRAIN AND HILARY'S FURIOUS WITH DARYL BECAUSE IT'S RAINING AND SHE'S LOST HER UMBRELLA.

THE DOMINIC SYSTEM IS ALSO GOOD FOR REMEMBERING DATES. TO REMEMBER THE YEAR IN WHICH ABRAHAM LINCOLN WAS ASSASSINATED, CONVERT 1865 TO ADOLF HITLER AND STEFAN EDBERG. NOW PICTURE ABRAHAM LINCOLN SITTING IN THE THEATRE WHERE HE WAS SHOT. ADOLF HITLER IS GOOSE-STEPPING ACROSS THE STAGE BEING CHASED BY STEFAN EDBERG, TENNIS RACKET IN HAND.

TIP: YOU DON'T ALWAYS NEED TO VISUALIZE THE FACE OR PHYSICAL APPEARANCE OF A PERSON. SOMETIMES A KEY ASPECT OF THEIR PERSONALITY, A FAMILIAR HABIT OR A PROP – SUCH AS STEFAN EDBERG'S TENNIS RACKET – IS ENOUGH TO TRIGGER AN IMAGE OF THAT PERSON.

THE COMBINATION APPROACH

All of the techniques I've covered so far will enable you to remember a wide range of facts and figures. But if you want a super-efficient way to remember long lists of things, particularly numbers, it's a good idea to combine two or more of these techniques. I find the DOMINIC system combined with the Journey Method particularly effective.

ACCORDING TO THE US CENSUS BUREAU, THE
CURRENT PROJECTED POPULATION OF THE WORLD
IS 6,254,821,715 (THIS FIGURE INCREASES
BY THE SECOND!). TO REMEMBER A NUMBER OF
THIS SIZE YOU NEED TO BREAK IT DOWN INTO
PERSONALITIES AND THEN GIVE EACH ONE A
PLACE OR A "HOME" IN A STRICT ORDER.

HERE GOES:

SAMUEL BECKETT (62 – SB)

ELIZA DOOLITTLE (54 – ED)

HUMPHREY BOGART (82 – HB)

ALEC GUINNESS (17 – AG)

ALBERT EINSTEIN (15 – AE)

NOW VISUALIZE A
TOUR AROUND
YOUR HOUSE OR
APARTMENT FROM
THE FRONT DOOR TO
YOUR BEDROOM –
MAKE SURE THERE
IS A SET SEQUENCE.

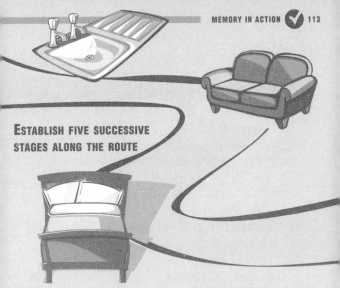

Establish five successive stages along the route

(Let's say that these are five different rooms — the kitchen, the dining room, the lounge, the bathroom and your bedroom). >

AT THE FIRST STAGE YOU MEET SAMUEL BECKETT (62). HE IS SAT AT YOUR KITCHEN TABLE HUNCHED OVER THE MANUSCRIPT OF HIS FINAL PLAY. PERHAPS HE'S EVEN ACTING IT OUT — MAKE THE IMAGE AS VIVID AS YOU CAN.

MOVING ON TO THE DINING ROOM, YOU SEE ELIZA DOOLITTLE (54). SHE'S MAKING A HUGE FLOWER DISPLAY IN THE MIDDLE OF YOUR DINING TABLE.

IN THE LOUNGE, HUMPHREY BOGART (82) IS SITTING ON YOUR COUCH IN HIS TRADEMARK HAT AND RAINCOAT, WATCHING OLD MOVIES ON YOUR TV.

NEXT, IN THE BATHROOM, ALEC GUINNESS (17) IS PLUNGING THE BASIN WITH A LIGHT SABRE (DRESSED AS OBE-WAN KENOBI IN STAR WARS).

FINALLY, YOU WALK INTO YOUR BEDROOM AND THERE, COMBING HIS LONG BEARD AT YOUR DRESSING TABLE, IS ALBERT EINSTEIN (15).

TRACE THE JOURNEY SEVERAL TIMES. WAIT FOR **30** MINUTES AND THEN REPLAY IT — THIS TIME CONVERT THE CHARACTERS BACK INTO NUMBERS. WHAT IS THE WORLD'S POPULATION? CHECK YOUR ANSWER AGAINST THE FIGURE ON PAGE **112**.

THE **DOMINIC** SYSTEM AND THE JOURNEY METHOD ARE FINE FOR REMEMBERING NUMBERS THAT CAN BE DIVIDED UP INTO PAIRS, BUT WHAT HAPPENS WHEN YOU NEED TO REMEMBER A NUMBER WITH AN ODD AMOUNT OF DIGITS?

FOR EXAMPLE: 23,358

IN THIS CASE, YOU GET TWO CHARACTERS (BILL CLINTON AND CLINT EASTWOOD) AND ONE DIGIT LEFT OVER – AN 8.

THE WAY TO TACKLE THIS IS TO COMBINE THE **DOMINIC** SYSTEM WITH ANOTHER METHOD, SUCH AS THE NUMBER–SHAPE SYSTEM (OR THE NUMBER–RHYME SYSTEM IF YOU PREFER).

SO, IN THIS CASE, YOUR MEMORY AID COULD BE BILL CLINTON GIVING CLINT EASTWOOD INSTRUCTIONS ON HOW

TO BUILD A SNOWMAN. A SNOWMAN IS THE SHAPE THAT
RESEMBLES THE NUMBER 8.

PRACTICE MAKES PERFECT!

NOW THAT YOU ARE FAMILIAR WITH MY SPECIALLY-DEVISED MEMORY TECHNIQUES, MAKE IT PART OF YOUR ROUTINE TO PRACTISE THEM REGULARLY — IN THIS WAY YOU WILL UTILIZE AND EXPAND YOUR MEMORY CAPACITY. YOU WILL SOON RECOGNIZE WHICH MNEMONIC METHODS SUIT YOU BEST. FOR EXAMPLE, IF VISUALIZING A FIGURE IN NUMBER—SHAPES IS YOUR STRENGTH MAKE SURE THAT WHEN YOU CREATE YOUR OWN COMBINATION APPROACH YOU INCORPORATE THE NUMBER—SHAPE SYSTEM.

THE MORE YOU PRACTISE THE ART OF ASSOCIATION THE MORE NATURAL IT WILL BECOME — YOU WILL BE PERSONALIZING MY METHODS IN NO TIME AT ALL! ONCE YOU ARE ACCOMPLISHED AT THINKING IN VISUAL SYMBOLS, YOU CAN REMEMBER ALL KINDS OF COMPLICATED FACTS AND FIGURES WITH EASE. MAYBE WE'LL MEET AT THE WORLD MEMORY CHAMPIONSHIPS!

ACKNOWLEDGMENTS

AUTHOR'S ACKNOWLEDGMENTS

I WISH TO THANK THE CREATIVE TEAM AT DUNCAN BAIRD PUBLISHERS, INCLUDING ZOË STONE, JUDY BARRATT, BOB SAXTON AND DAN STURGES, FOR PRODUCING THIS BOOK, AND ESPECIALLY KESTA DESMOND FOR HER INVALUABLE WORK.

EDITORIAL CONSULTANT: KESTA DESMOND
MANAGING EDITOR: JUDY BARRATT
EDITOR: ZOË STONE
MANAGING DESIGNER: DAN STURGES
DESIGNER: ADELLE MORRIS
COMMISSIONED ARTWORK: MAGGIE TINGLE